THE GIFT OF BLARNEY

A humbling story of hope and humanity.
—**Kate Durrant**

***

There were a lot of factors that had to line up that morning for David and they did; he had someone very special looking out for him "up there."
—**Ger O'Dea**

***

The fifteen minutes that David Motte does not remember are fifteen minutes that I will never forget.
—**Phyllis Dickinson**

***

When I met David and then interviewed him for our television channel in Ireland, I realized I was looking at and talking to a real-life miracle. The book is a must read for believers and non-believers.
An inspirational story of a man who beat all the odds.
—**Paul Byrne**

THE GIFT OF BLARNEY

Life, Death and a miracle atop a 600-year-old Castle

"The fifteen minutes that David Motte does not remember are fifteen minutes that I will never forget."

David B. Motte

Published by KHARIS PUBLISHING, an imprint of
KHARIS MEDIA LLC.

Copyright © 2024 David B. Motte

ISBN-13: 978-1-63746-228-7
ISBN-10: 1-63746-228-X

Library of Congress Control Number: 2023945715

All KHARIS PUBLISHING products are available at
special quantity dis- counts for bulk purchase for sales
promotions, premiums, fund-raising, and educational needs.
For details, contact:

Kharis Media LLC
Tel: 1-630-909-3405
support@kharispublishing.com

TABLE OF CONTENTS

Introduction 9

Planning the Trip of a Lifetime 11

Our Scheme Begins to Unravel 15

Back on Track 21

Blarney 29

Kate and Deborah 35

Hailey and Tonille Evans 39

To the Blarney Stone! 41

In Joy's Words 45

Hailey, Jessica and the Frenchman 47

Jessica Weirdht 51

Siobhan Hogan 55

In Joy's Words 57

Jeremy Downey 59

Ger O'Dea 61

Kate and Grainne 65

In Joy's Words 69

Irish Coast Guard Helicopter R115......................*71*

What Do I Remember?.. *73*

Recovery.. *79*

In Joy's Words... *85*

Release *87*

Return to Blarney!....................................*91*

In Joy's Words... *97*

Putting the Pieces Together.............................. *99*

Whose Plan Was It? *101*

Concluding thoughts. *107*

INTRODUCTION

On April 20, 2018, at the 600-year-old Blarney Castle in County Cork Ireland, I received a most precious gift. Not the gift of eloquence from kissing the Blarney Stone – I never made it to the top of the castle. I received the gift of God's incredible love and comfort, delivered through a diverse group of people from all over this globe.

I was given the Gift of Blarney.

And to all the wonderful people involved, I owe my life. From the depths of my soul, I share this story with love and thankfulness.

David Motte

PLANNING THE TRIP OF A LIFETIME

Joy, my bride of 34 years, had always wanted to travel to Ireland, experience its rich history, tour the unique ancient architecture, and view the splendor of the country's scenic landscapes. With camera and photographic equipment in hand, she longed to explore the diverse and beautiful countryside, tour small, quaint villages, and travel along the narrow winding roads to experience first-hand the people and culture of this intriguing country. And after years of talking and dreaming, it was finally time to put the wheels in motion.

We had recently become "empty nesters." Our three sons were grown and living on their own. A couple of years earlier, we'd sold our large empty house packed with the previous 15 years of memories of raising a family, but it had become too big for just the two of us. We were entering the next phase of our lives. Why not start it with a trip to celebrate our new-found freedom? Let's go to Ireland!

The timing seemed perfect, and we began gathering information to work through the details of what taking such a trip would require. Joy and I mapped out our itinerary well in advance with the hopes of creating a unique experience – a venture packed with new sights and sounds to share with family and friends through countless stories and the thousands of pictures she would be capturing with her camera. What a fantastic opportunity to create new memories to warmly reflect on and cherish for the remainder of our lives.

As we planned our trip, I insisted we stay in the best hotels, taste the best cuisines, and experience the finest that Ireland had to offer. Everything had to be top-notch and first-class to ensure our adventure was not a disappointment. With a rental car secured, GPS in hand, and reservations at key hotels (and castles) along the way, we would explore Ireland to our hearts' desires. I had everything in control.

In my mind, this would be a milestone in the timeline of our lives together. My best-laid plans were all coming together. I intended to spare nothing to create a perfect vacation abroad. My intentions were sincere, but not realistic.

Let's be honest. Best intentions aside, it is impossible to create perfect circumstances and experiences that we can "magically" store in our hearts and minds. Our most treasured and precious times in life are often anchored by sweet, tender memories and experiences from unique places and circumstances with the people we love dearest. These "moments" always come unplanned and unrehearsed - occurring when people, situations, and places collide or come together during spontaneous events that are often out of our control.

As Joy and I planned our trip, little did we know what lay ahead of us. We were not aware that years before we began planning this adventure, other details were developing; other people were making decisions that would impact our trip well in advance of that day, April 20, 2018.

A poem by Robert Burns, *To a Mouse* (1785), comes to mind that states, *"The best-laid schemes of mice and men go often askew, and leave us nothing but grief and pain, for promised joy!"* Or, as a friend of mine once said, "Just when you think you have everything in control, it becomes obvious that we are in control of nothing."

Someone much more significant and grander than us is well in control of the "best-laid schemes" of our lives, whether we admit it or not.

Unknown to Joy and me, a collision of circumstances and people in an incredibly unique place and time was about to occur.

OUR SCHEME BEGINS TO UNRAVEL

Our original plans were to travel to Ireland in March 2018 in time to celebrate St. Patrick's Day but, due to busy schedules and the urging of our travel agent not to travel around St. Patrick's Day, we decided to move the trip forward to mid-April 2018. After months of planning, our final itinerary had us departing Charlotte Douglas Airport in North Carolina on April 15, 2018, at 2:30 PM, with a stopover at Dulles Airport in Washington, DC. We would board another plane later that day and fly all night to our destination, Dublin, Ireland.

Arrival time in Dublin would be at 10:00 AM on April 16, 2018. While there, we would stay two nights at the Merrion Hotel with plans to take a self-guided sightseeing tour that would give us the freedom to explore and experience the history and culture of this 12th Century city at our leisure.

On April 15, 2018, we began our "trip of a lifetime." The drive to the airport was quick, with little traffic and no congestion. We parked our car in the long-term lot and boarded the shuttle bus which dropped off our luggage and us at the designated gate.

There were no delays as we arrived at the airline terminal with plenty of time to check our baggage, go through security, and make our way to the boarding gate.

The flight from Charlotte to Washington/Dulles airport was uneventful. Our next flight would take us to Dublin, where our real journey would begin, but due to severe weather, we spent the evening of April 15 in Dulles airport, anxiously waiting for the weather to pass. After our first delay, we finally boarded our plane and taxied to our place on the tarmac to wait our turn to take off. There, after a lengthy delay and little movement, our pilot informed us that we would taxi back to the terminal to let the storm pass and to pick up several more passengers from other connecting flights.

As we got off the plane, the airline assured us we would be leaving in an hour or two after every passenger from other connecting flights had arrived. Three hours later, we finally reboarded the aircraft and taxied out to the runway, only to hear the captain break in over the cabin speaker, "We have another storm coming through and will need to wait on the tarmac until it passes."

Another hour later, our plane returned to the terminal, because it was too late for us to take off safely. As we got off the plane AGAIN, we took our place in one of the long lines that had formed – trying to get information on the next flight to Dublin. At that point, I began to wonder if we were ever going to get to Ireland. And, as Joy and I suspected, the airline announced that all trips to Ireland had to be re-booked the following day.

We were given vouchers for a nearby hotel and as we walked through the airport to find our transportation, a dear couple came alongside us and struck up a conversation. They had come from County Cork, Ireland, had been vacationing in the United States, and were booked on our same flight for their return home. We shared a shuttle to the hotel and discovered they were just as eager to return home as we were to start our vacation in Ireland.

Early the following morning, with less than two hours of sleep, we headed back to the airport to board our new flight with the hope of arriving in Ireland sometime on April 17. Finally, more than 24 hours after our departure from Charlotte, NC, we boarded our plane in DC for the seven- and one-half hour flight to Dublin.

The airplane was packed – every seat full and elbow room a nonexistent commodity. Most of the passengers seemed restless, and we assumed they had missed the earlier flight as we had. As a result, it was challenging to sleep or rest during the long trip overseas. Joy and I were exhausted from the delays, filled with sleepless hours of anxiety and stress.

The long flight to Dublin was uncomfortable, with our arrival nothing more than a complete blur. Our plane landed and we made our way to the baggage claim and then through customs. I vaguely remember getting into the taxi that would take us to our hotel. It was early in the morning, and we could barely make out the city of Dublin as our driver navigated through the dark, narrow streets.

Joy and I arrived at the Dublin Merrion Hotel around 5:00 AM on April 17, with just enough time to check-in, settle in our room, and lay down for a couple of hours to try and get some much-needed rest.

The fact that we were in one of the most beautiful hotels in Dublin didn't matter. Fatigue overwhelmed us. We were still processing all the events of the day before. It was nice to be able to lay down on a luxurious bed with quality amenities, but a comfortable cot with a hard pillow would have been just as good. Too much travel, excitement, stress, and worry. So much for my best-laid plans.

After a couple of hours spent tossing and turning while desperately trying to sleep, we decided to get up and prepare for our first full day in Dublin. We had purchased a "stop-bus tour" (hop-on-hop-off) through our travel agency in advance. While the complete tour only lasted 90 minutes, it gave us the freedom to "hop" off the bus, explore parts of Dublin that looked interesting, then "hop" back on another bus as we moved from point to point throughout the city. Our destination was the Guinness Factory, where we would tour seven floors of the history of this famous landmark in Dublin.

What a whirlwind of new surroundings and learning to navigate the city of Dublin, all of which made for a hectic first day. But we made it to the Guinness Brewery to do the tour – seven stories and seven flights of steps, each revealing the city's history, culture and people. While ascending to every floor and passing through each exhibit, I couldn't believe how exhausted I felt, still trying to recover from our hectic travel itinerary.

We stopped in at a local pub that evening to have our first big meal in Ireland. Joy ordered fish and chips, and I had shepherd's pie, which are basic staples in Ireland. So much for fine cuisine and dining, but our food was delicious. Joy and I, both weary, decided to return to the hotel and get some much-needed rest.

The following morning, after another restless night with little sleep due to all the excitement, effects of jet lag, and time zone changes, Joy and I ate breakfast at the Merrion Hotel restaurant. It was there that I had my first encounter with blood sausage. This breakfast staple is made from pork, pork blood, and oatmeal and is quite common on most Irish breakfast menus. I must admit that, initially, I was not impressed with its taste and texture, but this would not be my last encounter with this local delicacy.

Although we were still tired, our appetites were satisfied, and we were finally back on schedule.

BACK ON TRACK

After breakfast, Joy returned to our hotel room to finish packing our bags, and I hailed a cab to take me to pick up our rental car. We were about to begin our trek across beautiful and intriguing Ireland. This was the moment our real adventure would begin.

We live in the United States of America. The steering wheels in our automobiles are on the left side of the car, and we drive on the right side of the road. In Ireland, the steering wheel is on the *right* side of the car, and, as every decent Irish person knows, you drive on the *left* side of the road. And, because many of the small cities and towns in Ireland are untouched by time, the streets are very narrow and very tight. Dublin is certainly not the best place in the world for a driving lesson on how to navigate on the wrong side of the road, in a different seat of the car, when traffic and pedestrians are coming at you from every direction.

I would never admit this to anyone (and I certainly did not tell Joy), but the experience of riding in a cab to pick up our rental car and my subsequent solo drive back to the hotel on the left side of the road through the busy streets of Dublin was, to put it mildly, one of the most stressful, white-knuckled, gut-wrenching experiences I've had in a long time. I had been driving for over forty years in the US and needed to figure out how to reverse everything in my mind from a directional point of view, but being an adrenaline junkie, I must admit it was fun.

I arrived back at the hotel in one piece, met Joy in the lobby, and with feigned confidence assured her that I knew how to navigate the left side of the road from the right side of the car through the narrow streets of a completely unfamiliar city, in an unknown country. I don't think she believed me for a second.

We loaded our luggage and, after receiving helpful suggestions from the hotel porter, headed down the eastern coast of Ireland toward Wexford on the first leg of our journey.

This drive would take us through the heart of the Wicklow Mountains to experience some of the most incredible landscapes in the country. Although the roads were very narrow, the traffic was light and allowed me to adjust my driving patterns and habits.

Once we arrived in Wexford, it was time to grab lunch, put gas in the car, and reset the GPS to take us to Kilkenny. The trip to Kilkenny was full of new experiences and taking in the countryside dotted with quaint villages along the way. Whenever Joy spotted a village, stream, or even a church building of interest, I would stop the car so she could take as many pictures as her heart desired. These moments began to reveal to us the beauty of Ireland. On more than one occasion, we stopped the car as cattle or sheep were crossing the road.

We had reservations that night at the Pembroke Hotel, which included a gourmet dinner and time to relax, regroup, and prepare for the following days' adventures. The gourmet dinner was wonderful, but I found myself craving another helping of shepherd's pie. It became obvious that our most dear moments would be the simple exposure to the people and unique culture of this wonderful country.

I laid my head on the pillow that night and remember thinking I had never felt so completely worn-out in my life.

Early the next morning on April 19, we found a small coffee shop in Kilkenny where we tried to work through our fatigue, shake the cobwebs from our heads, and plan the day's events. We had been traveling nonstop since April 15 and were tired and disoriented. It was almost impossible to get much sleep with the constant activities and trying to adjust to the five-hour time difference between Ireland and Charlotte, North Carolina.

Joy and I enjoyed our walk that morning through the quaint town of Kilkenny that seemed so untouched by time and displaying a long and unique history. The storefronts were colorful and neatly stacked on crooked streets that ran in every direction. Pubs dotted each block and offered a resting place for all who wanted to sit for a spell.

Then we made our way to the Kilkenny Castle and spent several hours touring the rooms and grounds. In just one morning, we were trying to take in the town, people, and culture that dated back more than eight hundred years. Of course, as in Dublin and Wexford, we had to stop and taste the local cuisine. We found a quaint pub to rest our feet and have lunch.

Our next stop was St. Canice's Cathedral, also known as the Kilkenny Cathedral, a 13th Century church with round-headed stained-glass windows and wonderfully unique marble floors. Next to the cathedral was the St. Canice's Tower, which is the oldest standing structure in Kilkenny City. Weather permitting, tourists can climb the round tower to enjoy magnificent views of the city. Rising 121 steps and one hundred feet high, St. Canice's Tower is one of only three round towers that people can explore in all of Ireland.

As we labored up the steep, wooden steps of the tower, I began to wonder if it was worth the pain involved to get to the top. I completed my climb of the tower's vertical steps out of breath and just in time to hear an Irish gentleman at the top say to Joy, "Now's a suitable time to get rid of him if you want to!" I'm sure Joy wouldn't have had to push hard to get my tired body over the thin rail.

Irish humor!

After stopping in another local pub to rest and rehydrate, we returned to the Pembroke Hotel to pick up our car. Next stop, County Cork, a two-hour trip southwest of Kilkenny, where we had reservations at the Hayfield Manor Hotel. The drive to Cork was mostly highways that were wide and easy to navigate, with one exception.

In Ireland, roundabouts (traffic circles in the US) control traffic at intersections. From an American point of view, imagine driving a car on the left side of the street while sitting on the right side of the vehicle and entering a traffic circle from the opposite lane and direction. Not a comfortable situation to navigate. Oncoming traffic moves from the right and is traveling to the left, and to make it more difficult, when exiting the circle, you must remember to stay on the left side of the road. For an American driver, this is not good.

Navigating those roundabouts turned out to be an incredibly unique process for us. I would begin by reminding myself that I was about to enter the circle from the left side of the road into the left lane with the intention of turning left at the proper junction. Joy would also verbally remind me to stay left, travel left and turn left during the full process. My intentions were to safely navigate the circle. Joy's intention was simply to survive. We fortunately lived to tell the story.

Navigating the narrow, thin streets up to Hayfield Manor was also stressful. Joy was convinced I would eventually destroy one or both of the car's side mirrors. The roads were steep and narrow, and I was relieved to see the hotel as we topped the final hill with cars lining both sides of the cramped street. By good fortune, a vacant parking spot (with our name on it) was open near the entrance, and I breathed a heartfelt prayer of thanks as we parked our car.

Hayfield Manor sits on two acres surrounded by beautiful gardens. Cork is a short and leisurely walk from the hotel. The charming coastal towns of Kinsale and Cobh, and the world-famous Blarney Castle, are a quick and scenic journey by car from the hotel.

After checking in, we walked towards the town of Cork in search of a small pub where we could get a bite to eat and prepare for the following day's activities. We had reservations the next morning to catch a paddy wagon Tour bus in Cork and spend the day touring Cobh and Blarney.

Cobh sits on an island in Cork city's harbor. It was the Titanic's last port of call in 1912, before its fateful first voyage. Blarney is a village just outside the city of Cork and is famous for its 600-year-old castle and gardens. On top of Blarney Castle is a piece of stone called the "Blarney Stone," said to give the "gift of gab" to all who kiss it.

During the planning stages of our vacation, I quickly made it known that my crowning achievement during our trip would be to climb Blarney Castle and kiss its magic stone. That was all I asked for or expected from the trip; everything else would be simply icing on the cake. It must have been the intrigue of the stone and excitement of traveling to a distant land to conquer this mystic legend. So, when asked what I wanted to do in Ireland, my response was always, "I want to kiss the Blarney Stone."

BLARNEY

Nestled in the town of Blarney in Cork County Ireland there's an old castle that has drawn the attention of people from across the globe for hundreds of years. Its history dates to the 13th Century when a wooden house was constructed on the site; the house was surrounded by sharpened sticks protruding from stacks of stones for protection. A stone fortress was built in its place around 1210, but it was destroyed in 1446. Cormac Laidir MacCarthy, the Lord of Muskerry, rebuilt the castle, which, in its ruined state, still stands today.

At the top of the castle, a "stone of eloquence" is embedded in one of the extending walls and is famously known as the Blarney Stone.

There are many stories about the beginnings of the Blarney Stone. According to the Blarney Stone website, *"some say it was Jacob's Pillow, brought to Ireland by the prophet Jeremiah. Here it became the Lia Fail or 'Fatal Stone,' used as an oracular throne of Irish kings – a kind of Harry Potter-like 'sorting hat' for kings. It was also said to be the deathbed pillow of St. Columba on the island of Iona. Legend says it was then removed to mainland Scotland, where it served as the prophetic power of royal succession, the Stone of Destiny.*

When Cormac MacCarthy, King of Munster, sent five thousand men to support Robert the Bruce in his defeat of the English at Bannockburn in 1314, a portion of the historic stone was given by the Scots in gratitude – and returned to Ireland.

Others say it may be a stone brought back to Ireland from the Crusades – the 'Stone of Ezel' behind which David hid on Jonathan's advice when he fled from his enemy, Saul. A few claim it was the stone that gushed water when struck by Moses." (https://blarneycastle.ie/blarney-stone/)

Neither the castle nor the stone's origins are entirely precise, but both exist today as one of the top twelve tourist sites in all of Ireland. In the past several years, over 450,000 people have visited Blarney Castle annually. It continues to lure hundreds of thousands of curious spectators to make the winding, narrowing, steep climb up a smoothly worn stone staircase of 185 steps that spiral 125 feet to the top of the castle.

Legend tells us those who are willing to climb the winding spiral stone staircase to the top of the castle, sit on a ledge in front of the Blarney Stone, contort their bodies by leaning backward over an opening ninety feet above the castle floor, and kiss the stone will then acquire the gift of eloquence. Whether this is true or not (and more than likely not) one cannot help but be drawn to the down-to-earth, peacefully quiet town of Blarney and the magnificent gardens surrounding its castle. And who cannot accept the challenge to climb the narrow, steep castle stairs and kiss the stone, while taking lots of pictures to show friends and loved one's evidence of this great adventure.

So, on April 20, 2018, with great anticipation and excitement, Joy and I left the Hayfield Manor Hotel to make the two-mile trek through the streets of Cork to rendezvous with our tour group at the St. Patrick bridge and begin the day's excursion. We walked through the beautiful city, carefully navigating unfamiliar new streets while constantly checking our tour map to make sure we would arrive at our destination on time. Once we found the tourist shop, it was not long before our paddy wagon tour bus pulled up to the curb where everyone was waiting.

We scheduled a half-day tour from Cork City to visit the two most famous towns in the region: Blarney and Cobh. Admission to Blarney Castle was part of the tour package, and there was plenty of time set aside to explore each town and enjoy the scenic drive through the beautiful Cork countryside.

Upon boarding the bus, we met Phyllis Dickinson and her husband Ron from Mattoon, Illinois. Phyllis and Ron were in Ireland to tour County Cork and, on a whim the previous night, had decided to check if there were openings for a trip to Blarney to visit the castle the next day.

Traveling with them was Jessica Wierdht, a veterinarian from O'Fallon, Illinois, who had been friends with the Dickinsons for many years. Jessica later told us again that the decision to go to Blarney was completely unplanned. The night before, they decided to walk into a tour shop just as it was closing and inquire about tours available for the area. We were grateful for the company, and Joy struck up a conversation with Jessica as the bus pulled away.

It's always fun to meet fellow Americans when traveling overseas – there is an instant bond, and it's interesting to discover what part of the States they are from and hear their thoughts of the new culture and people. Our new-found friends were there to tour Ireland and partner with us as we explored Blarney Castle and its surroundings. Little did we know what role they would play during the day's events.

Our frenzied trip to Ireland was beginning to take a toll on me. For five days and nights, our time had been consumed by dealing with delayed airline flights, treks through airports and customs, taxi rides, buses, and constant walking. We spent each moment touring and exploring every street while trying to process the incredible sights and sounds of an unfamiliar culture. Joy and I traveled a total of 3,718 miles across multiple time zones. From the moment we landed in Ireland, we had been going nonstop from one town to the next, one site to another, trying to make up time due to travel delays. It felt like we were continually trying to catch up to get back in control of our planned schedule.

Little did we know that our time in Ireland was already intricately planned. We were on God's itinerary, not our own. We were right on time. It was at this point that people, places, and plans from the past several years started to come together.

KATE AND DEBORAH

In mid-2015, Kate Durrant, a long-time resident of Blarney, received a phone call from Deborah Lynch. The two ladies had never met or talked before. In Kate's words, "I heard a hesitant voice over the phone as she introduced herself and said that Martin O'Shea had given her my phone number and told her that I would be interested in helping to raise funds to purchase a portable defibrillator for the village of Blarney."

Deborah worked in the coronary care unit of Cork University Hospital. She was genuinely concerned with the pattern of people coming into the cardiac unit who could have been revived but did not survive the initial trauma.

Kate, who is highly active in the Blarney community, lives just up the hill from the castle. The vista from her backyard is magnificent with a direct view of Blarney Castle and grounds. Most nights, the castle is majestically lit in bright lights for all to see. A resident of Blarney for twenty years, she has found her piece of "heaven."

After a brief first meeting with Deborah, Kate wandered off to do some fundraising and phoned Deborah a few weeks later to tell her that she had the funds secured - thinking that was all she needed to provide. "Great," said Deborah, "that's the easy part done." What Kate didn't realize was that Deborah had big plans. She wanted Kate to help her establish Blarney as a first responder community - having seen too many preventable deaths as people were rushed into the cardiac unit at Cork University Hospital with little or no immediate intervention from the local community.

Deborah and Kate took it upon themselves to organize their scheme by informing and educating the public citizenry of the lack of first response capabilities. Their plan was simple – mobilize and train a dedicated group of volunteers while challenging the community to step up to meet this critical need in Blarney. It was a need that, when fulfilled, would have an immediate impact on the whole community and provide a vital, lifesaving resource not only for the people of Blarney, but also for the thousands of people from all over the globe who came to visit and kiss the stone.

Kate and Deborah's decision to help make Blarney a first responder community would directly impact my life.

In October 2015, Kate, Deborah, and the volunteers known as the "first responders," a tight team of fourteen people (most of whom are still involved today) went live, which simply meant they were open for business - prepared and ready to help the Blarney community in its times of need. And, in Kate's words, "This didn't happen overnight. It's tough to get to the National Ambulance Service in Ireland to allow/certify you because of the intense training required for certification. On top of that, monthly training is required without fail. If you miss three months of continuous training, your certification is revoked. If you miss three separate months of training, you're out. No room for passengers, which is as it should be."

Deborah and Kate worked diligently in the Blarney area to make sure that volunteers were trained and equipped with the tools that they needed in first aid and CPR because of the history of accidents, of people having heart attacks, or needing some type of critical help. They wanted to make sure the Blarney community was prepared. There are less than 20 ambulances in all of County Cork, which means the response time during a critical event is high, and the survival rate is extremely low. They had been on a mission for over five years and have implemented a multi-layered solution for the Blarney community and, of course, the castle.

As Deborah and Kate became involved with the first responders of the Blarney area, they headed up a drive to get as many local people trained as first responders as they could. Blarney Castle had also trained its staff as first responders, which meant they were well versed in CPR. Due to the first responder's diligence, Blarney Castle also became the recipient of vitally needed portable defibrillators. If an emergency occurred, they could take care of people who were in dire need of life-saving support.

In the past, people had suffered life-threatening events on the steps of Blarney, and their fate was not a pleasant one. So, Blarney Castle had strategically placed defibrillators around the castle and posted signs to inform the public that Blarney Castle and its staff stood prepared.

HAILEY AND TONILLE EVANS

Two sisters from Aurora, Illinois, Hailey, and Tonille Evans, decided to take a 15-day trip to tour Ireland and Scotland together. Their original schedule was to fly to Ireland, visit the countryside, and then travel down to Scotland to complete their tour. Shortly before their adventures were to begin, their travel agency called them. There had been unavoidable changes in availability, and the agency asked if they could shorten their trip to 13 days, start their journey in Scotland, and finish traveling through Ireland 12 days later.

As part of the rescheduled trip, they ended up in County Cork and the town of Blarney on April 20, 2018. Hailey and Tonille boarded their tour bus that morning for the drive to Blarney Castle, where they would tour the grounds, climb the stairs, and kiss the famous Blarney Stone.

As the two sisters walked up the trail to Blarney Castle, Hailey, a police officer with the Lisle, Illinois Police Department, noticed one of the signs posted on the Blarney grounds informing the public there were AED (Automated External Defibrillator) devices available on the castle grounds. Thanks to Kate and Deborah, Blarney was officially a first responder community and had strategically placed these devices in the event someone had an emergency which required immediate attention. Hailey said she remembered making a mental note of the fact that the Blarney Castle grounds crew and staff had been trained and equipped with defibrillators in case of an accident.

TO THE BLARNEY STONE!

One of my most vivid memories on the morning of April 20, while walking through the streets of Cork, was thinking how physically exhausting the trip had been. Everything seemed blurred and distant. It had been difficult to sleep the night before, due to the hectic pace filled with constant travel and excitement. We did an enormous amount of walking the first three days as we toured Dublin and drove through the Wicklow Mountains making multiple stops along the way. The drive from Wexford to Kilkenny was stressful, given my determination to keep our car on the right side of the road (which was the left side).

During this incredible whirlwind of new sights, sounds, unfamiliar surroundings, and new people, I had not been drinking enough water and was becoming dehydrated. Nor had I been eating well. Unknown to me, this combination of diet, activity, and lack of sleep had caused my potassium levels to drop dangerously low. Plus, I was overweight and out of shape. Climbing a steep set of castle stairs was the worst thing I could have done that day, even though I had survived climbing the Canice Round Tower the day before.

As our tour bus arrived, we boarded, and I quickly found a seat, relieved to sit down and rest from our long trek through Cork. At this point, time started to become surreal to me. It wasn't long before our paddy wagon was winding through the streets of Cork, making quick time on its way to the town of Blarney.

The conversations on the bus sounded like distant echoes, and I vaguely remember looking out the window as we approached the castle grounds and passed through the entry gates. As the bus came to a stop, I recall seeing the souvenir shop at the castle entrance. From this point on, my memories became blurred and dream-like.

I have fuzzy recollections of getting off the bus, walking past the souvenir shop, and making my way toward the castle. There are small bits of memories while I strolled up the pathway that leads to Blarney Castle – seeing the green foliage that was so beautifully kept on the grounds and walking on a bridge to cross over a small, gentle stream.

I can also remember seeing a stone with a round hole cut in it for pictures of the castle and seeing Joy walk up to the stone with her camera. For the rest of that day, I have no memories, except for a 15-minute period of time in Blarney Castle.

In retrospect, something was physically happening to me during the walk to Blarney Castle. Strangely, it seemed like my mind was beginning to detach from my body – my feeling of reality was starting to shift. I am quite sure now that I was in physical distress.

Time and memories stopped for me as we neared the castle. Joy told me that we entered the castle and began to climb the narrow, spiral staircase cut in stone and slowly ascend to the top of the castle. I have no memories of entering the castle or beginning the climb up the narrow, rain dampened steps to kiss the infamous Blarney Stone.

And then it happened.

Two-thirds of the way up the castle stairs, I collapsed. My heart had stopped beating. I was in full cardiac arrest.

IN JOY'S WORDS

*W*hen David's cardiac arrest happened, we were about two-thirds of the way up the castle steps which are narrow and winding. As we headed up the steps, a couple of people had filed in behind me, and David was following them. So, due to the curve of the staircase, I couldn't see him as we climbed the steep stairway. About two-thirds of the way up, I heard someone yelling "help." At first, I had no idea it was David who needed help.

David had collapsed on the narrow spiral steps leading to the top of the castle. A couple of tourists were holding him to keep him from falling further down the staircase as they called for help. His heart had just stopped. I remember vividly hearing and trying to process their words that there was no pulse.

The tourists quickly responded and maneuvered David down a flight and a half of stairs to get him to a flat area to perform CPR. It happened that a young police officer from Lisle, Illinois had just kissed the stone and was heading down another staircase on the opposite side of the castle. She heard the yells for help, rushed over to help, and immediately began CPR.

HAILEY, JESSICA AND THE FRENCHMAN

Hailey and Tonille toured the grounds of Blarney Castle, enjoying the beautiful arrays of trees, shrubs, and flowers, and then walked to the castle to climb the stairs to the Blarney Stone. As they climbed up the dark, winding staircase to the top of the castle, they couldn't help but feel a sense of claustrophobia within the gently narrowing stairway. Once at the top, they made their way around the castle roof with the rest of their tour group to get in line to kiss the Blarney Stone.

After kissing the stone and enjoying the views from the top of the 600-year-old castle, Hailey and Tonille made their way toward the exit stairway with the rest of their group to leave the castle. Their tour guide had reminded them that they had two hours to tour the grounds and explore the castle before heading off to the next destination, and time was running out.

It was at this point that Hailey said, for some reason, as they made their way towards the exit stairwell, she became interested in an informational plaque and stopped to take a picture with Tonille at the top of the stairs. While she was reading the plaque, the rest of their group descended the steps and exited the castle.

After one final picture, the two sisters started down the steps to catch up with the rest of their group. Hailey thought she heard someone yelling for help as they entered the staircase, and just as she asked Tonille if she heard someone calling for help, another scream for help came from somewhere within the castle.

Tonille said at this point, without hesitating or thinking, Hailey handed her coat, phone, and pocketbook to Tonille and quickly began to make her way towards the sounds of the desperate pleas. She crawled under a chained-off area to somehow find a path that would take her across the castle towards the urgent calls for assistance. Hailey navigated her way through a narrow passage and began maneuvering through a slit in the wall to the spiral staircase that led up to the castle roof. As she entered the opening, she saw my lifeless body collapsed on the castle stairs.

An elderly gentleman had positioned himself under my shoulders to try to keep me from falling further down the castle steps, but the sheer weight of my limp body was too much for him to manage. At that point, Hailey reached down to check and see if she could find a pulse in my wrist or neck. There was none.

I had fallen backwards so that my head pointed down the steps, and my feet were pointing up the steps. She immediately noticed I was taking agonal breaths, which were my body's reflexes gasping for oxygen. Hailey wasn't sure if I had hit my head during the fall and was concerned as to the extent of any injuries I might have incurred during the collapse and fall.

When a cardiac arrest victim's heart stops pumping blood due to a disorganized rhythm, the breathing center in the brain begins to starve for oxygen-rich blood. Time is extremely critical at this point. Every second is precious, and minutes can determine the difference between survival and death.

She knew that she needed to somehow position herself below my body to stop me from falling further down the steps and to check for signs of a pulse and breathing. Still, the narrowness of the staircase and the position of my body made it next to impossible. The only solution she could think of was to jump over my body on the stairs and try to land on a small stone step below my head.

Knowing the situation was critical and that time was precious, Hailey was about to launch herself over my lifeless body when a young man appeared on the steps below me and said he was able to help. And to Hailey's amazement, this young man happened to be a paramedic from France on vacation in Blarney.

The young paramedic checked for signs of a heartbeat and proclaimed there was no pulse. Both

Hailey and the Frenchman had been trained for situations like this and knew they would need to get my body positioned on a flat surface before they could start administering CPR. Hailey said that she "was very acutely aware that time was passing, and my chances for surviving were quickly running out."

A cardiac arrest victim's brain cells start dying within 4-6 minutes of losing blood flow. Each minute afterward, the chances of restoring those brain cells drop by approximately 10%. After 10-16 minutes, the cardiac arrest victim is functionally brain dead.

These two young professionals somehow managed to pick me up on the steep, narrow passageway and maneuver my limp, heavy body down a flight and a half of steps through a narrow opening in the wall that led to a small room that provided access to a flat area inside the castle. At that point, they quickly positioned me on my back to begin CPR.

JESSICA WEIRDHT

Jessica was climbing the castle steps that day with Joy just ahead of her. The two had struck up a quick friendship on the paddy wagon ride to the castle and were continuing their conversation as they ascended the winding steps together. As Joy reached the top of the castle and began to exit the stairwell, Jessica heard cries for help and quickly looked back but couldn't see what was happening below her. Jessica was concerned that Ron Dickinson might have had difficulties with the narrow castle steps and wanted to make sure that he was OK.

As she walked down the steps, she saw me slumped against the wall and noticed my breathing appeared to be agonal breaths and immediately knew time was of the essence. Jessica yelled to Joy that I had collapsed and was injured.

As Hailey and the French paramedic appeared on the scene, Jessica assisted them and helped carry me down the steep steps in search of a flat area. The stone steps of the castle are narrow and exceptionally smooth due to hundreds of years of wear by the elements and foot traffic. That morning, they were slightly damp from rain the day before. I have no idea how Hailey, the Frenchman, and Jessica were able to move my lifeless body down those steps, but this brave group of three was able to maneuver me to a flat location, position me on the stone castle floor, and start administering CPR.

Jessica made sure my airway was clear and began performing mouth to mouth resuscitation for breathing. Hailey began to count and started chest compressions while the French paramedic was constantly checking for a pulse and voluntary respiration during the process. After four rounds of CPR, there was still no pulse, and I was not breathing on my own. The average "round of CPR" lasts two minutes. Time was running out. Every second was critical, and the situation did not look good for me.

Hailey later said she was keenly aware that my condition was becoming more critical by the minute, but she also said that she felt an intense determination and was not going to stop until she got my heart beating again and "bring me back."

They performed six rounds of CPR with no results. My heart would not restart. Time was running out for me and most involved with the effort did not think I would survive.

As all of this was taking place, Phyllis Dickinson, fully aware now that I had collapsed on the castle steps, grabbed her phone and dialed 911 to try and summon help. The call went through, and the operator asked her where Blarney Castle was. Of course, Phyllis did not know the physical address of the castle. Still, somehow the call went through to the right place at a critical time and notified the first responders of Blarney, and someone placed a call from the Blarney staff down to the courtyard that they needed a defibrillator.

Phyllis later shared with us, "I remember Jessica quickly putting her hands together as in praying and signaling me to get around your body and the three first responders (Hailey, the French paramedic and Jessica, the veterinarian) with Joy to pray...I guess I was in the communications department that day with phone in hand and prayer on heart."

Phyllis' communication had set off another chain of events on the castle grounds.

SIOBHAN HOGAN

Siobhan, an employee of Blarney Castle staff, was on site on April 20, working around the coffee shop area where a portable defibrillator was hanging on the wall. She was part of the Blarney Castle team and had received training two weeks prior in first-aid, CPR, and how to use the AED defibrillator. Thanks to the commitment of the first responder community and castle staff, if someone needed immediate aid during their visit to the castle, this team was well-trained to act quickly.

As the call came through that a tourist was in distress on the castle steps, Siobhan was standing next to the defibrillator. She quickly grabbed the portable device and ran to the castle steps, steps that were crowded with tourists going up to kiss the Blarney Stone.

Siobhan arrived with the defibrillator as the group continued to struggle to administer chest compressions, breathing, and monitoring for any signs of life. Still nothing.

They quickly attached the leads of the defibrillator to my chest and turned on the AED. No pulse or rhythm registered on the device screen. It instructed the responders to provide an electrical shock to me – and Hailey yelled for everyone to clear.

An AED delivers a 3000-volt charge in less than 0.001 of a second. That is enough electricity to light a 100-watt bulb for 23 seconds. The unit then instructs the user to begin CPR right away. After two minutes, the unit will perform another analysis to see if defibrillation is needed again.

For obvious reasons, due to the extremely high voltage, no one must be touching the victim who is about to be shocked. Jessica noticed that Hailey's leg was touching my arm and quickly made sure she was clear. The team administered a shock through the defibrillator, and, after a long second, the machine picked up a rhythm.

We have a heartbeat!

For at least 15 minutes, my heart stopped and remained still. Was it now capable of carrying a normal rhythm after so much time had passed? Did enough oxygen flow through my brain to keep it functional? Were my internal organs capable of functioning after such an extended amount of time? As paramedics arrived on the scene, there was discussion to determine if they should shock me again or if CPR needed to be continued.

IN JOY'S WORDS

*I*n the meantime, a call had gone down to the castle staff, and a young lady from the staff grabbed a defibrillator and ran up the castle steps, which was not an easy task. She had trained to do CPR and use a defibrillator just two weeks before our visit!

David was, in all reality, dead. I vividly remember how he lay there with his eyes glazed over and the continued phrase that there was no heartbeat from those working so hard to revive him. I don't think anyone thought they would be able to revive him, but after about twelve minutes of CPR and shocking him with the defib, he responded. Those were wonderful words then, "We have a heartbeat."

I stood there watching all of this. God provided sweet people, both castle staff and tourists, who took turns with their arms around me as we stood there. It was surreal. My thoughts were running the gamut of possibilities: Would his heart continue to beat? Would there be brain or organ damage after so long a time? What do I need to do from here to get home from Ireland alone?

But through all these thoughts, God's presence and overwhelming peace were obvious. It is hard to describe, but I KNEW whatever the outcome, it would be OK. God was in control.

57

JEREMY DOWNEY

Jeremy Downey is an active member and leader of the Blarney first responder team. He had started a new project with Downey Cleaning the morning of April 20 on the grounds of Blarney Castle, just yards away from the scene. As the alarm went out, Jeremy hurriedly made his way up the castle steps. He knew all too well how critical each moment was during this type of trauma.

"The first four to six minutes a person goes into cardiac arrest are the most important. After that, the heart no longer has a shockable rhythm. An ambulance will take longer than six minutes, which is why first responders are so critically important," he said.

Jeremy arrived on the scene and began to coordinate the first responders, paramedics, and a growing number of castle staff who came to my aid.

He was no stranger to situations like this. Over the years, Jeremy has often been first on the scene for emergencies of this type and diligently worked to save lives. Many of those emergencies involving his close friends and people of the Blarney community did not have the positive outcome that mine did.

Jeremy has described his role as a first responder as a way of giving back to the community. "My own father, Con, was shocked back to life back in 1999 while in Cyprus. Eighteen years later, he is still with us, and his experience is what pushed me to get involved in Blarney First Responders."

GER O'DEA

G er O'Dea has over 23 years of experience as a firefighter and paramedic in County Cork. On the morning of April 20, 2018, he was in a nearby town taking care of personal business just 10 minutes from Blarney Castle.

In Ger's words, "This is the only reason I was less than 10 minutes from the castle since I live over 30 minutes away." He received a text from ambulance control that there had been an incident at the castle and quickly drove over. Ger had been an off-duty responder for more than fifteen years and was acting entirely on instinct.

As he arrived at the castle, Ger was directed to my location in the castle and arrived seconds after I had received a shock from the defibrillator. Not comfortable with my breathing pattern, he instructed that Hailey perform another cycle of CPR which instigated a discussion regarding the value of continuing. He was off duty but had his ambulance radio with him and was able to give updates to ambulance control as they approached the castle and me.

The paramedics arrived, and hurriedly began to try and stabilize me. As I struggled to regain consciousness, they decided to sedate me to alleviate more stress on my heart. At this point, Ger began to determine how to get me out of the castle. He made requests to the fire service and a rescue helicopter but was informed the rescue helicopter could not come. Two years earlier, Ger had responded to Blarney Castle for an incident like mine and it was deemed unsafe for the rescue helicopter to respond due to the possibility of flying debris being a hazard.

On that occasion, once they stabilized the patient, the paramedics were barely able to maneuver the gurney and patient down the narrow steps. Since I was much larger than she was, there was no way to get me out of the castle.

Ger remembered having been told by a friend who was a helicopter paramedic to insist that a call be put through to the Coast Guard if that ever happened again, and the Coast Guard would come and assess the scene. Ger made the call to request the helicopter and ensured it was passed to the Irish Coast Guard. Within 25 minutes, Irish Coast Guard Helicopter R115 was hovering overhead preparing to winch me up in a gurney.

He later told me, "*Until that day in Blarney, I never in all my career stepped up and made myself presentable as the lead in a successful call but on this occasion, I can say that following the excellent care you received prior to my arrival, the advanced medical care delivered by the paramedics and advanced paramedics at the scene, that I used my previous experience and inside knowledge to get you out of there successfully. In a coordinated effort between the paramedics on scene and the fire service and first responders, you were stabilized, secured, and transferred to the area from which you were winched up."*

KATE AND GRAINNE

Every weekday morning at 9:00 AM, Kate Durrant and Grainne McSweeney met to walk through one of the best-kept secrets outside of the town of Blarney. The castle sits amid a beautiful piece of real estate in County Cork complete with rolling hills, gentle streams, and a fantastic array of trees, vibrant green plants, and rainbow-colored flowers.

The grounds surrounding the castle are beautifully maintained and meticulously well kept. All who visit can experience the beauty of nature and take in the peaceful and tranquil scenery Blarney has to offer. The history behind its winding trails, stone walls, streams, and buildings runs more than six hundred years long, and to stroll amongst the Blarney Castle grounds is an experience unto itself. Those who walk it for the first time cannot help but think they have been transported to another place and time – a world full of peace, tranquility, and beauty.

It was in this setting, weather and schedules permitting, that Kate and Grainne met each morning for their walk, to talk, laugh, and share life's experiences in what was already a strong, enduring friendship between these two dear ladies of Blarney.

It was a significant part of their busy schedules, a time to breathe deeply and prepare for the day's activities since both were highly active with their families and within the Blarney community.

For no particular reason, on April 20, 2018, they were unable to make the usual time and canceled their daily walk, but Grainne was convinced that Kate had something on her mind and needed to talk. Kate will tell you that this was not the case, as she had nothing on her mind. After much insistence on Grainne's part, they decided to meet an hour later that morning; Kate and Grainne met a little before 10:00 AM that morning because each of them felt they needed to be available for their friend.

And, in Kate's words, "Except for this day, they had NEVER adjusted their time to take their morning walk, nor have they since then."

As they walked through the winding paths of the Blarney Gardens outside the castle, it became starkly clear something had happened. They heard the deafening sounds of large engines roaring and rotor blades beating in the air and looked up to see a Coast Guard helicopter hovering high above the castle. Kate and Grainne started taking pictures with their camera phones as the helicopter began to slowly descend closer and closer to the top of the castle.

But when a first responder emerged from the aircraft tethered to a gurney on a winch and cable and was slowly being lowered to the castle floor, it was apparent the situation was complicated. Kate knew that an accident had occurred and had a sinking feeling in her stomach as she and Grainne both knew, more than likely, it was not a good thing.

As Kate and Grainne rounded one of the paths outside the castle, they watched the helicopter rescue team slowly winch up a patient on a gurney out of the castle and onto the helicopter. They realized that it was taking quite a long time for them to get everything organized to get the victim out and felt that it wasn't going to be a good news story at all.

The helicopter then rose high above the castle and maneuvered to a field beside the castle to land. They both had stopped taking pictures because everything was moving so slowly, and they felt that it was going to be a tragic ending. Once on the ground, no one was rushing to get the injured tourist to the hospital. When the helicopter crew and paramedics transferred the patient to the ambulance, they shut the door, but they did not drive off with speed to the hospital.

Kate and Grainne presumed that there was nothing more that could be done for this person and began to walk again. As they walked up the main path to the castle, there was another ambulance parked beside it, and Kate noticed a woman sitting on the passenger side.

Kate said to Grainne, "I wonder if this person is involved with the accident?"

Neither of them knew it was Joy waiting in the ambulance to go to the hospital with me. Kate and Grainne both were hesitant because they didn't want to interrupt or disrupt this person. If she was part of the first responder crew, she was there for a reason.

As they came up to the ambulance, Kate and Grainne looked at each other and agreed they should check in on her.

Kate looked through the window and noticed the lady's nails were "very prettily done." At that moment, she realized that this woman was connected to the incident that had just occurred. And Grainne, being the go-getter that she is, at once reached down to grab the handle of the door of the ambulance and opened it to ask Joy if she needed help. They were very gracious to Joy, offering her their help and providing their phone numbers to her. Both ladies left Joy with the promise that they would check in on her at the hospital.

IN JOY'S WORDS

The rescue took quite a while. The Coast Guard sent a helicopter because there was no way to get a gurney down the castle steps. The helicopter lowered a rescuer to the rough stone floor of the castle opening where David was laying. They secured him in the gurney and winched him to the helicopter. They carefully set him down on the castle grounds so that they could transport him to the hospital via an ambulance.

It was while I was sitting in another ambulance waiting that the door of that ambulance was opened by two Irish women – two wonderful women whom I have absolutely no doubt that God provided that day. These two women regularly walk on the grounds of Blarney Castle early in the morning. For some reason --God-- that day, they walked later in the morning, which they never did. These ladies reached out to me, a total stranger, and wanted to help in any way they could. I stayed in their homes during David's hospitalization. They provided transportation for me back and forth to the hospital as needed, fed me, and did everything they could to help. It was amazing we forged deep friendships in such a brief time. It was all according to God's plan.

IRISH COAST GUARD HELICOPTER R115

My incident created a unique set of circumstances. During a later media interview, Joy said, "You would think that having a cardiac arrest at the top of a 600-year-old castle would be the worst place, but it turned out to be the best."

Besides, had all the people involved not been in the right places during the precise time, it would have been my last day on this earth. Ger O'Dea's insistence that his call be put through to the Irish Coast Guard provided the only solution to evacuate me from Blarney Castle both safely and quickly.

Irish Coast Guard Helicopter R115 responded to the call that day. This highly trained team lives in quiet humility as most first responders do. Their response was quick. The helicopter hovered over the castle less than 30 minutes after the call went through. The rescue was not easy. The natural downdraft created by the helicopter's huge rotors posed a safety risk to the castle. Stones laid six hundred years before were often worn and brittle, and the wind forces created by the helicopter could cause damage to the castle and the people below who were committed to the rescue.

The brave men and women of ICGH R115 bravely positioned the helicopter over the castle and lowered a first responder on a cable down to the main surface of the castle. Once in the castle, the responder had to make sure I was secured in a metal gurney, attach it to a cable along with himself, and keep the gurney stable while it was winched up to the helicopter for transport. This team performed their rescue flawlessly and then gently touched down in a field beside the castle so that the ambulance could take me to Cork University Hospital.

This was the first time such a rescue had been performed at Blarney Castle, and it was perfectly executed with no damage to the castle or to the patient.

WHAT DO I REMEMBER?

It is overwhelming to think of the incredible set of events that were successively occurring, with every second counting and each minute more critical than the one before. Looking back, I do not doubt that God was in control of every intricate detail as He guided people, circumstances, and events. All of those involved felt His presence. His hand was evident through the brave and selfless acts of individual people and well-prepared service groups.

During my collapse in Blarney Castle, I passed from life through the gateway of death. My understanding of its purpose and nature radically changed. Death is unavoidable and inevitable for all of us. My experience at the Blarney Castle confirmed the absolute inevitability of death. We will all eventually face its reality. We may choose to ignore it and attempt to escape it but, in the end, must all face it.

> *"Everyone has to die once then face the consequences"*
> (Hebrews 9:27 The Message).

We have no control over the timing or manner of our introduction to death. There was nothing ugly or alarming about the entire experience to me. Dying was smooth and peaceful – a subtle and natural transition of consciousness and reality - not a sudden jolt or disruption like we face on this earth. I was moving to a place and toward someone I knew I belonged to. I was on a journey home—a return to my origins. And there was a clear and unmistakable awareness that I was being ushered toward the presence of the God who conceived and made me.

Death is the passage that takes us back to God. It is a mystery simply because most of us will only pass through it one time during our earthly existence. But death is final from an earthly perspective. It is always sudden and shocking. No matter how we prepare for it, the reality of it leaves us empty and hurt. The results of death on this earth are sobering and final. This is what is called the "sting" of death.

I was aware of having passed to the other side and very clearly knew that my existence was not in the world I was accustomed to. I was experiencing a peace that, to this day, I cannot fully describe or completely comprehend. An utterly overwhelming peace that I long for to this day.

So, as I think back and try to piece together the fragments of my memory that exist of that day in Ireland, it is essential that I separate what I was *told* and what I have *read* from what I experienced during that period of my physical collapse. Those memories are intensely vivid and bright, but I remember nothing more. One thing that I am sure of is that my experience was in the heavenly realm.

My consciousness instantly adjusted to my new surroundings, and it was evident that I had no control over my destiny from that point forward. I had transitioned from an earthly reality that afforded me the freedom to make decisions and remain completely in control of my daily existence. No more. I found myself in a spiritual reality that was completely out of my control and totally centered on God.

One unarguable truth became very clear. There is absolutely a God who is absolute. He is the center and source of everything. He is eternal and without limits. I transitioned from a world of uncertainty to a reality where God is central and certain. He does not change.

Time did not define the reality that I lived in during those earthly minutes of my physical distress. Although it seems so inadequate, I can only try to put into words all the incredible sensations and feelings, truths, and presences I experienced during those moments. It is impossible to describe the eternal in the temporal realm we live in today. That part of my experience in Blarney will take some time to process and convey the details of passing from the temporal world we live to an eternal reality beyond.

Time had stopped for me. It was non-existent. I was wrapped in eternity.

The reality of Heaven and eternity is infinitely richer than the reality of this earth. Since my ordeal at

Blarney Castle, I have not felt at home on this earth. Don't read this the wrong way. Life since Blarney Castle has been full, exciting, and challenging even through its difficulties. But there is a Heaven, and I am convinced God wants all of us to spend eternity with Him there.

At the very center of Heaven and eternity is a God who completely and infinitely loves us. His love is deeper and purer than any human condition we experience while living on this earth. Words cannot do justice to the all-consuming and infinite love of God. There is an absolute peace that emanates from the presence of God's love that to this day, I cannot find words to adequately convey its fullness and beauty.

"No one's ever seen or heard anything like this, never so much as imagined anything quite like it – what God has arranged for those who love him"
(1 Corinthians 2:9 The Message).

There was a precise point of my journey when I knew that this experience, as incredible as it was, had nothing to do with my physical death on this earth. My body may have died, but I was not dead. I was being held and cared for, but this was just a part of God conducting something on a larger scale. It wasn't about me; it was about the wonderful people contributing to the situation at hand. He was actively intervening through this situation, making Himself known in our human existence.

And that was the exact part of my experience when I became fully aware that time is not measured in God's presence, and I understood that I was not to pass completely over the bridge of death into an eternal presence with God. It was unquestionably clear in my mind that I would be returning to my body and life on earth.

It was not my time to go.

At some point I became conscious that He was going to send me back to the physical, earthly realm to which I was accustomed. I felt movement and experienced the sensation of being inserted back into my earthly body. I was no longer in eternity. I was back to the familiar. I immediately felt incapacitated.

My body jolted with an innate need to struggle and resist. Some may call it "fight or flight," but I was desperately trying to lift myself, trying to raise my head and move my arms and my hands to somehow gain control over my physical body, but I was unable to do so. And at that moment, an intense wave of fear completely enveloped and overwhelmed me. I had just left the most peaceful, incredible love that I had ever sensed and experienced, but was now bound to the physical realm I had left minutes before.

God's gentle, loving presence was, for the moment, gone, and I was trapped again in this body with no control over myself. I tried to lift my head and sensed the need to fight the overwhelming fear apart from God's immediate presence. I vividly remember moaning in terror and feeling that I was about to break down mentally and emotionally. I could not fathom a life apart from the God who made me and whose presence I had just left.

And then, very softly in my ear, I heard Joy's voice saying, "David, it's OK." I can hear it now in my mind as clearly as when she spoke to me while I was lying on the floor of Blarney Castle. At the same time, paramedics hovered over me desperately struggling to stabilize me, hoping to see a consistent heartbeat, a rhythm, pulse, or any sign of life.

Joy said one of the paramedics told her that I could not hear her, but another one encouraged her to speak to me, and I am so thankful he did. The moment I heard her voice, I became acclimated and consciously aware I was back in my earthly body. Her voice sounded like the voice of an angel. Her presence and comfort allowed me to relax and be at peace.

RECOVERY

My next memories are blurred and vague. I can remember moving on a gurney down a hallway in Cork University Hospital and asking questions as to my condition. I was aware of intense pain around my chest and rib cage and asked why I hurt. I remember asking if they had to perform CPR on me and inquiring if I had to be shocked. Having performed CPR on other people before, I was aware of how serious this situation must have been.

Joy said my response was, "Ooh, that's not good!"

I have fuzzy images in my mind of being wheeled to a room for an angiogram and remember seeing the monitors around me during the procedure. But that is all.

I later discovered that Deborah Lynch, who, along with Kate Durrant, was the driving force behind the Blarney first responders' scheme, was assisting the cardiologist who performed my angiogram and looked after me during my recovery. Her vision of a solution to the tragedies of people dying for lack of preparedness had become a reality.

What a coincidence? I think not. God does not operate coincidentally.

Deborah later relayed to Kate, "*On the day of the accident I was having my morning break when I looked at the phone to see that a cardiac arrest had come through but wasn't sure if someone had responded. I hoped someone had; my stomach always turns if we can't reach these patients. That's the aim of the scheme. I was working and due to be on call at the catheter lab for the weekend but kept enquiring all day and finally found out that he was brought to the coronary care unit and was stable. The plan was to perform his coronary angiogram the following day (Saturday). We knew we would be in to do his angiogram procedure that day.*

"*Seeing him that Saturday morning was a bit surreal - that he had survived. I felt a huge pride for our little group and Jeremy for stepping up to the mark, once again. Then the rest of the story unfolded… Joy being cared for by you and true humanity and humility at its best. The outcome we all aim for had become a reality: that this person who is someone's husband, father, son and brother gets a second chance to enjoy life.*"

Joy has told me that I repeatedly asked the same set of questions: "Why does my chest hurt?" "Did they have to shock me?" And I always responded, "Ooh, That's not good.

She did tell me that after the 20th time I asked her the same set questions in the same order, instead of giving me the same responses, she finally said, "David, we had a major argument last night at the hotel and I got the best of you."

My response? "Ooh, that's not good!"

I have a vivid memory of one evening in the hospital of seeing a man standing at the door of my room. He stated he had met us earlier and was checking in to make sure everything was OK. He told me that if we needed anything at all they would be there to help us. His visit was such a comfort to me and a testament to the wonderful and caring people of Ireland. To this day, I cannot remember who this dear man was. But his love and concern were such an inspiration during my recovery.

Joy relayed to me that the lovely couple from Ireland we met at Dulles Airport before arriving in Dublin had also stopped by the hospital. They were very gracious to Joy and wanted to make sure she had everything she needed. Their presence during this hectic time was a comfort to her, as well as another confirmation that God was in control of the events that transpired that day.

The next day, Joy came into my room in the CCU and described to me how helpful everyone in Blarney had been. A gentleman at our hotel had offered to work with the rental car company to have our car picked up.

Every time a word of thanks was offered up, the response was the same, "We're only doing what anyone else would do."

We were waiting for test results to determine my condition and any treatment that would be necessary. The hospital would provide a place for Joy to stay onsite until we knew what lay ahead of us.

Curtis Saunders, a dear friend of ours from the States, being told of the situation and thinking that I had not survived, quickly worked to secure plane tickets to fly over and help Joy work through returning home. He was glad to later receive a message from Joy that I had pulled through to live another day.

Our oldest son, Chris, was fervently trying to work out a plan to fly to Ireland and take care of us while keeping our other two sons, Evan and Corey, informed, along with family and friends. The responses and prayers of people from the States were overwhelming. The American Embassy in Ireland even called Joy on two occasions to offer their help.

What was a significant crisis to all involved, though, was not a crisis for me. In my broken memory, I had gone from walking toward an old castle with beautiful surroundings to riding in a gurney down a hospital hallway. Despite being well taken care of by those on this earth who fought to bring me back, I had no memories of the earthly event. Apart from the trauma of leaving the presence of Jesus when I was revived, there is no memory of the physical pain or discomfort I experienced during that time. It is as if I was being shielded or protected from the trauma. Even though my chest was painful and sore it didn't consume me. Emotionally, I felt no fear or anxiety, but instead was totally at peace.

The most incredible gift to Joy and me during the entire ordeal was the people of Blarney.

The following day, the hospital notified Joy that the boarding facility offered to families in need was not available, which was unusual. She remembered that Kate and Grainne had printed their names and phone numbers on a piece of paper and asked her to let them know if she needed anything. Joy decided to call Kate (the reason for this is that Joy did not know how to pronounce Grainne's name) to ask her where the best place to stay close to the hospital was, and Kate immediately replied, "You can stay with me." From that point on, these two wonderful friends from Blarney treated Joy like royalty. She stayed with Kate the first two nights and with Grainne on the third night of our ordeal. They supplied her with transportation to and from the hospital and any meals she needed. Every time Joy would thank them, their response was, "We're just doing what anyone else would do."

My test results were incredible. There was no damage to my heart. Dr. Ronan Curtin sat me down and explained the ordeal. He said the episode was like a lightning strike, and it would more than likely never happen again. My potassium levels had dropped dangerously low and short-circuited my heart. He said if I had come in for tests under any other circumstances, he would recommend treatment through medications along with a strict diet and exercise program. He informed me that he needed to perform a cardiac stress test, but if that turned out well, I could travel home to the States and finish my medical care there. I had no broken ribs or any other circumstances that would delay my travel home.

Scientists and doctors say that the human body has a built-in protective mechanism that does not allow one to remember details surrounding a traumatic event. It may be a way of protecting the mind and body of someone who has been through a harrowing situation and serves to alleviate any negative stress while the body and mind reorient and begin to heal. To this day, my memory has gaps about the incident at Blarney on April 20, 2018.

The survival rate of cardiac arrests occurring inside a hospital is twenty-four percent. Outside of a hospital, the survival rate is just six percent. Had I collapsed at the Canice Round Tower the day before, there would have been no chance of my survival. In almost any other circumstance imaginable, the odds of living would have been slim to none.

The first thing I remember hearing from Dr. Curtin was, "You really should not be here." I heard the same statement from my cardiologist in Charlotte, NC. As I became acclimated during the days and weeks after that fateful event, one fact remained vividly clear: A miracle occurred that day in Blarney.

I am reminded of Joy's words, "You would think that having a cardiac arrest at the top of a 600-year-old castle would be the worst place, but it turned out to be the best."

IN JOY'S WORDS

*D*avid was treated at Cork University Hospital. After a couple of days, he was almost normal as far as his heart goes. The doctors determined there were no blockages or damage to his heart. The testing indicated that a sudden drop in potassium caused his heart to stop. After more extensive testing, including a cardio stress test, the doctors' opinion was that he would be OK to travel back to the States as planned. So, we took the flight home, which we had originally booked.

The fact that David had survived with no heart or brain damage was nothing less than a miracle. Yet, the most incredible thing to David and me is what God did behind the scenes in the lives of those who were put in our path.

•

RELEASE

Cork University Hospital released me on April 24, 2018, just four days after I collapsed on the stairs of Blarney Castle. Joy informed me that Kate would be coming by to pick us up and take us to Grainne's home for a meal and time to regroup. It just so happened that PJ, Kate's "other half," had a test scheduled for the same day and time of my release from the hospital so Joy and Kate took care of the men in their lives together. Not a coincidence. God was present in every detail, and all involved became aware of His presence. During those three days, a deep bond had formed between Joy and these wonderful women who took care of her every need.

When Joy came into my room and told me of the plans to handle my discharge, she realized I had not met any of her new friends. My time was consumed with working through the traumatic event I had suffered physically, while mentally struggling to understand what had happened during the past three days. I trusted Joy completely and trusted Kate and Grainne.

Had it not been for these two lovely ladies with bold personalities, Joy would have been completely on her own in a foreign country. And my experience was that Kate and Grainne were every bit as lovely and caring as Joy had described, and more. Their hospitality was amazing. The most endearing quality of Kate, Grainne, and the people of Blarney was their willingness to give of themselves while thinking nothing of it. Only God could create this outcome.

Grainne and Kevin McSweeney had us to their home for a beautiful and delicious lunch with Kate, PJ, and Paul Byrne, a local reporter who had covered our story in the media. Even though I had just met them, these dear people seemed like old friends. I will always remember their love and hospitality, especially for taking care of Joy, who was over 3,700 miles from home in a strange country. There were no strangers at lunch that day.

Per Kate's suggestion, we had made reservations in Adare to rest for two days before flying home. It is a village in County Limerick with a population of less than 1,500 people and it's only a 30-minute drive from the Shannon Airport.

Adare's streets are lined with thatched cottages, and it is peaceful and quiet, presenting itself as a safe haven for weary travelers, which perfectly describes our situation. We had experienced an incredible set of circumstances and were ready to rest.

At her insistence, Kate would drive us the hour and a half trip by car to the Dunraven Arms Hotel. There we could relax and begin to process the amazing events of the past four days before flying back home. As Kate and Joy hugged and said good-bye to each other, it was obvious that God had formed a uniquely deep friendship between these two women over three days.

Joy and I took a short walk through the streets of Adare, but my energy level was low, so we stopped to get something to eat before going back to the hotel. I ordered blood sausage again and decided it would go on my "favorites" list. Fine dining.

As we walked out of the restaurant to head back to our hotel, we looked up to see a beautiful rainbow in the sky above, and one second later, it disappeared -- another sign of God's presence and provision.

On April 26, after driving an hour and a half from Cork, Grainne pulled up to our hotel and picked us up to take us to Shannon Airport. She wouldn't let us touch our baggage, drove us to the airport, and escorted us into the airport lobby to check-in. After Grainne's firm insistence that the baggage clerk take special care of us, we said our goodbyes with hugs and tears, then took our place in line to go through customs for the flight home.

During the long flight home, Joy and I spent our time talking through the incredible events of our trip and experiences. Neither of us could have imagined the journey God had planned for us in Ireland. Our best laid plans were irrelevant.

The media called it a tragedy with a good ending, but during that tragic event, God was present. He brought people together and built dynamic relationships through acts of love and kindness.

At one point during the flight, Joy looked at me and asked, "Knowing everything that happened the past ten days, and given that you could change nothing, would you do it again?"

My answer came without thought, "In a heartbeat, yes!"

RETURN TO BLARNEY!

Our flight back to the States was smooth and uneventful, thank goodness, and as we arrived at Charlotte Douglas Airport, Curtis Saunders was waiting to pick us up and take us home. He assured us that he would help us retrieve our parked car the next day. Our dear friend was determined to make sure we arrived home safely to get some much-needed rest.

The following weeks kept me busy with doctor appointments and more tests than I care to remember. Over three months, I'm certain they drew enough blood to clone another human being. My cardiologist was amazed at my condition but instructed me to change my diet and lose weight. As with all cardiac patients, I enrolled in a three-month rehabilitation program to ensure good habits became a natural way of life during the recovery period.

The more we settled back into our normal lifestyle, the more I felt like a part of me remained in Ireland. It had taken time to absorb everything that had happened during our "perfect vacation," but a couple of things continued to haunt me.

I always assumed the lost memories about the incident would gradually return. Other than random bits and pieces of my time in the hospital, everything about Blarney and the castle is still a total blank, but realizing how miraculous my survival was, I had a deep-seated sense of obligation that I needed to thank the people who saved my life. There were no memories of Hailey, Jessica, Ger, Siobhan, the Frenchman, or any of the others who gave so much and worked so hard to bring me back. I *had* to find and thank them.

While Joy and I were talking one day, we looked at each other and I said, "We have to go back!" The look in her eyes and smile on her face let me know she was thinking the same thing.

After three months of rehab, I lost fifty pounds, and my doctors became confident I was on the right track. I was free to do anything I wanted within normal limits. Apart from the time it took for my bruised ribs and chest to heal fully, there were no complications from the entire ordeal. It was time to go back to Ireland.

At that point, we did what anyone else would do. Joy retrieved the piece of paper she'd received from Kate and Grainne while sitting in the ambulance outside Blarney Castle. We called Kate to ask if she could help us coordinate a meeting with the first responders and Blarney Castle staff who were instrumental in my survival. Of course, Kate was all in for such a trip since she had a penchant for well-designed schemes.

The flight for our return to Ireland was smooth and uneventful - no storms or delays. We arrived at Shannon Airport full of nervous energy to be back in our newly- adopted country. After our customs check, we quickly gathered our baggage and went to pick up a rental car.

Yes, we were actually going to dare to navigate the wrong side of the road from the right side of the car once again. Joy was elated to discover that our car was equipped with sensors and alarms which would help to eliminate the chance of me destroying one or both of the car's side mirrors. She became my chief navigator every time we encountered a traffic circle – constantly reminding me to enter from the left onto the left lane while turning left to exit.

Kate had suggested we meet at Sheen Falls Lodge in Kenmare to spend a day getting reacquainted and prepare for our journey back to Blarney. We navigated the two-hour drive to the lodge and met up with Kate and PJ. It seemed as if no time had passed during the five months after April 20, 2018. It was a wonderful time to express our thanks and gratitude in less dramatic circumstances. It was also Kate's birthday, and we enjoyed a wonderful celebration with her family and friends.

We then returned to Blarney where Kate and PJ hosted us in their home. Kate had scheduled a time for us to return to the castle the following day. The owners and castle staff were so gracious and allowed us to visit privately with the staff and tour the castle before its doors were opened to the public.

My hopes and expectations were high. I was convinced it was possible to retrieve the time and memories lost on that fateful day. One thing remained constant in my mind: I was still determined to climb the castle steps and kiss the Blarney Stone.

As we arrived at Blarney Castle, Joy and I were met with a large contingency of the media and began our walk towards the castle. My heart was pounding; every beat felt as if it was bouncing off the walls of my chest. Would the memories start flooding my mind as we retraced the steps I had taken just five months before? As we walked over the small bridge toward the stone with a hole cut in it, things seemed more familiar, but as we walked toward the castle and entered the doors leading to the spiral steps, everything seemed strangely unfamiliar.

We met Siobhan Hogan at the base of the steps and were able to spend time with her as we began the climb up to the top of the castle. Still, there were no memories; nothing returned, and in essence, I was experiencing Blarney Castle for the first time.

It was humbling to look up at the steep and narrow stone steps of the castle as we began our climb to the top. I couldn't imagine how I could collapse on them without incurring some type of severe injury. My heart was still pounding, and I said a prayer of thanks that it was. We stopped two-thirds of the way up the steps at the exact spot where I had fallen unconscious when my heart stopped beating five months before.

Even though I had no recollection of those events, I became overwhelmed with gratitude for the incredibly wonderful people who were willing to risk their safety to take care of me and fight for me during a critical life and death event. I was completely filled with awe and humility.

Joy and I made our way to the top of the castle and were able to meet many of the people directly involved with saving my life. We were surrounded by reporters, cameras and the like, but managed to reach the Blarney Stone. After five long months, I sat on the carved stone ledge high upon the castle, leaned back while holding on to iron railings, and kissed the Blarney Stone! The words that followed were not eloquent but were a heart-felt, "Thank you!"

IN JOY'S WORDS

We went back to Ireland in September 2018 to thank as many of the Irish people as possible for all that they did. The media and Blarney Castle staff met us the day we went to climb the steps again, this time hoping and praying that we would ascend and descend the normal way! Although I have vivid memories of that April day, David had no recollection of even walking up to the castle; he didn't even recall entering the castle grounds or the beginning of the climb. As we approached the castle this second time, a few memories came back for him.

So yes, it was emotional – especially for David – to see the actual structure of the castle. He realized how difficult the rescue had been, and just what a miracle it was that he had lived. After talking with some of the people involved in the rescue, we were even more thankful to the first responders and God, of course, who had orchestrated every little detail that day according to His plan.

We realized even more how miraculous it all had been – not just for us but how God had made Himself known to all those who were involved. We were overwhelmed with gratefulness and affirmation that our God is so awesome and that He is ever so present in our lives and can make Himself known in such beautiful ways.

My new friend, Kate, was one of our biggest encouragers to share our story with the media. We were invited to appear on a national television show before we left Ireland the second time and had decided not to go on the show since we were on the east coast, and the studio was across Ireland on the west coast. But after she encouraged us to go, saying, "What better way to tell others about God's love throughout Ireland," we felt compelled to go. And we did.

PUTTING THE PIECES TOGETHER

After our return to the States, we traveled to Mattoon, Illinois to spend a couple of days with Ron and Phyllis Dickinson and Jessica Wierdht. We shared a lovely dinner of Mexican meatloaf *a la Jessica* with them and took time to reconnect and ask questions regarding that incredible day in April 2018. I was also amazed to hear the different perspectives and experiences that were shared that day. Everyone involved provided a specific need during the crisis.

I began to realize during our second trip to Ireland that there were so many people involved that day in April, each giving their time and efforts and playing a specific role in the drama that had occurred. My desire was to gather these details and clarify the efforts and actions taken during my collapse.

A few days later, we met with Hailey and Tonille Evans and were able to connect with them for the first time since that day in April 2018. Over dinner, we shared our gratitude and love for their life-saving efforts. It was incredible to hear the details of their experiences and feelings, and to begin to piece together the miraculous series of events that so quickly evolved during those brief moments.

I cannot convey the deep sense of love and gratitude I felt for the sacrifice and selfless acts these wonderful people were willing to endure to save my life. Without exception, everyone stated that they were only doing what anyone else would do.

Every person involved had a specific role in my survival – each person was positioned at a critical location during exactly the right time. Defibrillators were strategically placed around the castle grounds. Training and refresher courses were held on a regular basis. During months of travel, email communications, and phone calls to gather all the details, we realized that all of the participants during my collapse at Blarney Castle were only aware of their part of the puzzle. As we gathered all the pieces to uncover the tapestry that God stitched together that day, it was evident to us that we needed to share it with everyone involved.

WHOSE PLAN WAS IT?

We were initially supposed to travel to Ireland in March – one full month before our actual travel dates. Had we done so, the critical people and pieces would not have been in place. I now realize how my best laid plans were never part of this trip. We were never in control, God was.

The strange developments during our first two days of travel involving weather patterns, late boarding passengers, and flights canceled at the last minute set our plans on a new trajectory, one that was out of our control. All of this directly contributed to my physical condition and health issues at the castle. On April 19, Joy and I climbed up the steps of the Canice Round Tower which were harder and far steeper than those at Blarney Castle. There were only three of us climbing the round tower with no way to communicate in case of an emergency. If I had collapsed there, I would not be here.

So many people came together in a very brief amount of time. All our plans and agendas turned into God's bringing together a combination of people and events to create a miracle that only He could create. Had that not occurred, I would not be here today to share this story. Some might say it was coincidental, others might say it was fate, but I am convinced that God orchestrated all the details during that time on April 20, 2018.

God wants to be involved in our lives. We have the freedom to choose His involvement or ignore His presence every day.

Had any one of those pieces not been in place, the outcome would more than likely have been entirely different. And echoing in my mind, I can still hear Dr. Curtin telling me that "your experience was like a lightning strike. It would probably never happen again, and, quite honestly, you really should not be sitting in from of me here today."

It would be impossible to list all the details of that day in Ireland. I often tell those who ask that my part in this whole incident was simple. I collapsed and physically died.

The following are just a few of the many people who contributed to the Gift of Blarney and the unusual circumstances that placed them in the right place at the right time:

• Hailey and Tonille Evans should never have been at the castle on April 20, but due to scheduling issues, their travel agency asked them to adjust their itinerary. They decided to accept the new travel plans and ended up at Blarney Castle at the exact place and time on April 20, 2018. Without Hailey's immediate response and quick thinking, I would not have survived. She was determined to continue trying until my heart began to beat again.

- Jessica Wierdht and Phyllis and Ron Dickinson were not supposed to be at Blarney Castle that day, but on a whim the night before, stepped into a tourist shop and asked if there were any openings for tours the following day. Jessica, a veterinarian, responded quickly and professionally. She, too, saved my life. As we were having dinner together in Illinois months later, Joy asked Jessica if that was her first-time performing CPR. Her response, "Yes, on a human!"

- Siobhan Hogan was standing near a telephone next to a defibrillator when the call came down to bring it up. Had she been anywhere else on the grounds of Blarney Castle, it would have taken her much longer to retrieve the defibrillator and make her way to the top of the castle. Just two weeks earlier, she also had just completed training on how to use the defibrillator, and it was still fresh in her mind.

- Jeremy Downey, in his first day on the job, had started a new project on the Blarney Castle grounds the morning of April 20, which allowed him to be close enough to give guidance and support. The most endearing qualities possessed by Jeremy and the team of first responders are their love and compassion for others. Kate summed it up as follows: "It's a privilege to be with someone in their darkest hours. On January 10th I was blessed, with Jeremy, to be called to the home of one of my closest friends, Denis. Sadly, so sadly, he didn't live, but what a gift to be there."

• Ger O'Dea was only 10 minutes away from the castle because he received a call and had to take care of personal business in Blarney. Two years earlier as a paramedic, Ger had been the first to reach another person who had collapsed at the castle and he had orchestrated her rescue. Without that experience, he would not have known to push his request through to the Coast Guard helicopter to get them to come to the castle.

• Ger later told me, "There were a lot of factors that had to line up that morning for you, and they did. You have someone very special looking out for you up there." Without Ger's leadership and guidance, my transport to Cork University Hospital would have been dramatically delayed. His main concern throughout the ordeal was to make sure that the right steps were taken to ensure a positive outcome.

- One piece of this story has baffled me from the beginning: the appearance and contribution made by the paramedic from France. Had the French paramedic not shown up at the exact moment that Hailey Evans was preparing to jump over my lifeless body, there is no telling what would have happened to Hailey and how that would have increased the time needed to take care of my physical needs. He was also very instrumental in helping Hailey and Jessica carry my lifeless body down a flight and a half of narrow winding steps to a flat location in which they could perform CPR. Without his incredible contributions, I am convinced I would not be here today to share the story. To this day, we still do not know his name or any other details about him. Joy remembers seeing him in front of the ambulance she was sitting in, but after checking on my condition he was never seen again. I have always thought that he was my guardian angel from France.

- Kate Durant and Grainne McSweeney changed their daily walk for the first time on April 20, 2018. Kate said they never had, before, or since, changed the time they meet to walk around the castle grounds. When the boarding facility at Cork University Hospital became unavailable for Joy, she had nowhere to stay; she had checked out of the Hayfield Manor and walked to Cork University Hospital the day after my collapse. Her call to Kate for information was received with outstretched arms full of love and grace. Without this simple act of hospitality, Joy would have been on her own to find a hotel and transportation while I was in the CCU.

CONCLUDING THOUGHTS. . .

To this day, it amazes me to look back at all the details and how they came together in perfect order. People acted quickly and made split-second decisions, all intricately timed during each minute, every piece falling into its exact place. There is no way to explain in human words something that was orchestrated by the Divine.

The fact that I am writing this continues to inspire me because I am fully aware that what happened to me in Blarney, Ireland on April 20, 2018 was a miracle.

I will forever be indebted to the beautiful people who became voluntary participants during this event. The question will always remain in my mind: How do I thank so many people who are the real reason this story has a happy ending? I will never be able to answer that question until I return to the God of eternity who briefly held me that day.

What we experienced during our trip to Blarney was simply humanity at its best. I believe that all of us, from every part of the globe, are here for a reason. We all have ambitions, desires, and an innate need to be relevant as we walk through this wonderful gift we call life. We want to have a reason to live for and to discover where we belong.

The lesson I learned from Blarney was that we all have a purpose in life. Everyone matters. Everyone is a precious creation of the God who loves us all unconditionally.

We live in a world that is deeply scarred by rebellion – rebellion against the God who created us, against our world and everything in it. Throughout the ages, we have witnessed how that rebellious attitude divides, destroys and damages humankind, but throughout our existence two truths remain: 1) We have all been created in God's image and I am convinced that deep within our souls there is a deep need to love God and love others; and 2) God loves us, has never left us or let us down, and has prepared a way for us to fulfill that purpose through a personal relationship with Him. He wants to be intimately involved in our lives.

> *"How? You ask. In Christ, God put the wrong on Him who never did anything wrong, so we could be put right with God"*
> (II Corinthians 5:21, The Message).

God was intimately working in so many lives on April 20, 2018. Everyone involved has stated that an extraordinary chain of events revealed God's complete and unwavering love, and that love became evident as I received the gift of Blarney.

About Kharis Publishing:

Kharis Publishing, an imprint of Kharis Media LLC, is a leading Christian and inspirational book publisher based in Aurora, Chicago metropolitan area, Illinois. Kharis' dual mission is to give voice to under-represented writers (including women and first-time authors) and equip orphans in developing countries with literacy tools. That is why, for each book sold, the publisher channels some of the proceeds into providing books and computers for orphanages in developing countries so that these kids may learn to read, dream, and grow. For a limited time, Kharis Publishing is accepting unsolicited queries for nonfiction (Christian, self-help, memoirs, business, health and wellness) from qualified leaders, professionals, pastors, and ministers. Learn more at: https://kharispublishing.com/